Deliver Workshops That Bring in Clients

A How-To Guide for Coaches, Consultants & Entrepreneurs

D1532243

LESLIE ZUCKER

Limits of Liability and Disclaimer

The intent of the author is to provide ideas, suggestions, examples and worksheets that help you to deliver a workshop that brings in clients. The author and/or publisher do not guarantee that anyone following them, however, will become successful. The author and/or publisher shall have neither liability nor responsibility to anyone with respect to any loss or damage caused, or alleged to be caused, directly or indirectly, by the information contained in this book.

A Note From the Author

Like you, I care. I care about being helpful and con-
tributing in a positive way. My wish for this book is that
it will help you to contribute to the world in a positive
way as well.

What I do for a living, how I do it and whom I collaborate
with makes a big difference to me. I work hard, and I
love to play hard, too. Maybe you can relate? To be
grateful, helpful, and happy are the main ingredients
in my life. I'm grateful for this opportunity to share my
work with you and for your time and attention.

I have made a career out of helping people learn.
Sometimes that looked like organizing groups of
people to learn Spanish or dance, other times that
looked like delivering workshops for executives about
how people learn and how to inspire their employees to
change their behavior. I've traveled, lived and worked
in Latin America, Africa, Asia, Europe and the United
States noticing differences in teaching, training and
presentation styles and eventually landed on my own
style – it's light-hearted, informal, extremely practical
and includes physical movement. In this book, you'll
get a sense of that.

Although I am thankful for the opportunities I had
working with so many dedicated people on the
staff of non-profit organizations, non-governmental
organizations and private sector companies, I realized
that I am wired like an entrepreneur. Once I truly
owned that truth about myself, I set out to be one.
It gave me a sense of freedom to develop my own
services and express my own style. The lesson that
immediately followed, however, is that while it's my
opportunity, it's also my sole responsibility to take

advantage of that freedom.

At the same time, I realized how difficult it can be as an entrepreneur to find clients. Even with my self-awareness, talent and courage, I still didn't know how to market myself. I took the advice of well-intentioned friends and colleagues and began to offer services for free or highly discounted, as a way to find new clients. Or so, I thought. With this approach, I became increasingly frustrated. While I gained experience, I did not grow my client base by much, and did not see a sustainable future for myself. I worried. Again, maybe you can relate? Then I set out to learn marketing for entrepreneurs.

With a new understanding of marketing, combined with my wish to be helpful, I created a service that was more "me" than anything I'd done before. This service is a combination of many of my gifts and hobbies: training, facilitation, coaching, business, cross-cultural awareness, self-awareness and even dance and other forms of movement. I began teaching others to design and deliver their own signature workshops that bring in clients to their business.

At my first workshop on this topic, I converted 66% of the attendees into paying clients who hired me to help them create their own workshop! I knew I was onto something truly helpful for other entrepreneurs and with real potential for my business. I repeated my workshop every few weeks for the first few months and it quickly became my signature workshop. Now I've delivered it dozens of times for hundreds of people. It is called the same as this book, "Deliver Workshops That Bring In Clients."

At my workshops, I met people who, just like me (and

maybe you?) love to train and teach others, knew they were good at it, and wanted to use that gift to market themselves. I built my business by helping my clients design, develop and deliver their signature workshops to find their clients. Yet, as I was reaching a full practice, I realized that my workshops and private workshop coaching could not reach as many people as I wanted to help. That's why I've written this book. It is a written version of my private workshop coaching on how to deliver workshops that bring in clients.

My goal with this book is to make it so practical, helpful, and convenient that you want to keep it close at hand. I believe the worksheets alone achieve that goal, and that the rest of the content, including examples from people just like you and me, will exceed your expectations.

Even if you don't read this whole book, I suggest you scan the Table of Contents, the page called "If You Only Read This Page, Here are Five Things to Remember" and the section called "What Makes This Book Worth Your While." Those pages alone will be helpful.

If you do, in fact, find this book highly valuable and believe it could be helpful to other coaches, consultants and entrepreneurs, please share a copy with them. I hope it will help them, too. The more we can help each other, the better off all of us are, right?

That said, experience shows that we do not learn only by reading a book. Many times we understand a concept, theory or piece of advice, but when we try to apply it, we realize that it's much easier said than done. Remember the last time you tried to learn a new instrument, language or dance? The instructor likely made it look pretty easy. Then you tried it, and it wasn't easy at all. The same is true for creating a workshop that brings in clients.

As you read this book, and fill in the worksheets, you'll find the spots that are tricky for you. It can be paralyzing for some people. Please don't let that happen to you. Don't get stuck, get help! To create the right signature workshop, you need clarity, support, guidance, community, feedback and repetition. Unfortunately, that's more than this book can provide. Fortunately, it's what I provide! I can help you design your signature workshop, and successfully market it so the right people attend it and convert into clients.

When you're ready to invest in yourself by creating the right signature workshop that brings in clients to your business, I would love to help. Please be in touch!

In this dance of life together,

Leslie

Connect With the Author

If you enjoy this book, I am available to you or groups you're involved with to offer workshops and provide even more resources.

I speak at conferences, professional development groups, networking events, coaching courses, consulting firms, anywhere full of people who are responsible for marketing themselves and finding their own clients. Please reach out if you'd like to discuss a speaking engagement.

One participant of my workshop wrote:

Hi Leslie:

Thank you for your great workshop yesterday!

The 2.5 hours flew by as we all learned wonderful things from you. I am looking forward to exploring the gift packet that you sent out via email and implementing some of the ideas right away for a workshop.

Your advice is clear, simple and sound. I also really appreciate how you allowed all of us in the class to be ourselves- you encourage that instinctively.

I have felt that in too much of my education my professors have told me and fellow classmates to change completely at our very cores- "...just be like me!". Some things are good for us to change. However, it's also important for us to celebrate our individuality and to be true to ourselves.

Cheers to you!

I recommend you highly to anyone wishing to learn effective strategies to create an effective workshop for marketing purposes.

P.S. I love your stretches. I felt so much better afterwards.

That's exactly the type of response my work is designed to inspire. On my website, you can sign up for workshop coaching to gain the clarity you need to design your own workshop and the confidence to deliver it so well that your participants convert into clients.

To see what previous clients have said about working with me, visit my website.

While you're there, sign up for free video blogs in which I offer more worksheets, examples, tips and tricks about delivering workshops that bring in clients.

🌐 *www.lesliezucker.com*

🌐 *www.deliverworkshopsthatbringinclients.com*

✉ *info@lesliezucker.com*

🐦 *@DCWorkshopWoman*

f *facebook.com/lesliezuckertrainingandcoaching*

in *linkedin.com/in/lesliezucker*

TABLE OF CONTENTS

Acknowledgements

Thank you to the hundreds of people in the Washington, DC metropolitan area who have come to my workshops and to the clients who have trusted me and taught me so much. The opportunity to understand you, your gifts and struggles, made this book possible. It is truly an incredibly rewarding experience to help you help yourself.

Thank you, Fabienne Fredrickson, of The Client Attraction Business School and Boldheart Academy, for teaching me to market myself with integrity, authenticity and love. You inspired me to reach a larger audience and have a greater impact in the world by writing this book. I am enormously grateful for your loving challenge to do so.

Thank you, Kimberley Jutze, for the irreplaceable input, advice and feedback. You helped me to see what was missing from this book and to write a much more helpful book than it would have been without you.

Thank you, Catalan Conlon, for the excellent editing and encouraging feedback.

Thank you, Kelly King, for the hugely positive influence you've had in my life, as we seek to help people sit less and move more. Your beautiful and sincere nature comes out in surprisingly welcomed ways.

To my parents, Bill Zucker and Susan Zucker, thank you for your care, love and support all these years.

Lastly, to Ben Homola, my partner and love, thank you for your limitless thoughtfulness, encouragement, and patience. Like so many lucky people who have crossed your path, I am a far better person because of you.

If You Only Read This Page, Here are Five Things to Remember

1. Be able to describe what you want to sell as a result of your presentation or workshop. Describe the problem it solves, all the value that it offers, all the benefits that people will get from it, all the reasons why it's important and timely.

2. Be able to describe the future clients you'd like to get as a result of your workshop. Describe people who recognize that working with you is crucial to solving their problems, already know that they need your help, are easily identified and contacted, get great results from working with you, happily pay what you're worth and refer other clients to you. And, most importantly, choose people you really enjoy working with!

3. In the title and the short description of your workshop, convey the specific benefits to a specific kind of person with a specific problem. When those people read it, they will identify with the description, give up other plans and show up for your workshop. That's who you want there...*pre-qualified prospects*.

4. As entrepreneurs, our job is to protect our confidence. While it's important to protect it every day, it's especially important to find your confidence and keep it during your workshop. An audience can "read" confidence, or lack of it! Lacking confidence in front of your audience will not lead to the results you want.

5. Many people who offer workshops don't follow up or stay in touch with workshop participants over time. Follow-up is a necessary ingredient for converting your audience into paying clients.

What Makes This Book Worth Your While

As a self-employed coach, consultant or entrepreneur, you likely want to grow your business by finding new clients. You have valuable skills and could genuinely help people, if only they knew about you and your products or services. That's the challenge. People don't know about you. Or, at least, not enough of the right people know about you.

You've probably heard the expression, "It's a numbers game." You want to increase the number of people that know about your business and increase the number of people in your pipeline or sales funnel. You turn to public speaking or a workshop for more visibility.

You are a confident public speaker, experienced trainer and practiced facilitator. You love to teach or train people – maybe you're a former teacher or the one who always got asked to teach other people something. You are not afraid to speak in front of an audience, when you are clear about the topic and have no doubt you can help people. Sure, you might still get a little nervous before an event, but you have techniques to turn your nerves into enthusiasm.

Over the years, you have welcomed and enjoyed opportunities to give presentations or lead workshops, trainings, events, or speeches.   Throughout this book I will refer to them as workshops since I prefer a participatory style that includes time for the participants to apply or "to workshop" the concepts to their own situation. Likewise, in this book I offer worksheets so you can apply the concepts I offer to your own situation.

You know how much time it takes to create a fantastic workshop. You're familiar (maybe far too familiar) with the questions that come up in the process. Many times, you don't have a clear answer to your own questions, so you reluctantly make a choice just hoping it's the right one. Sometimes it is and sometimes it isn't.

You are acutely aware that the time to create a workshop is unpaid time. It requires focus, persistence, dedication and concentration. It's time away from paying clients, friends, family and your social life. Maybe you've already offered various workshops and experienced the disappointment of low interest, low attendance, or low conversions – meaning that your audience didn't convert into paying clients. Or, maybe you were successful in getting people to your workshop, and into your sales funnel, but then, after the workshop, they jumped right back out of your sales funnel again, and follow-up with them was fruitless or impossible.

For all these reasons, I believe that creating workshops is far too much work to NOT bring in clients from them.

This is why I suggest that you focus your time and attention on one workshop- the RIGHT workshop. Some people call this a "Signature Talk" because it's what they become known for. Toastmasters calls it a "Back Pocket Speech".

It should provide incredible value to your ideal clients, be unique to you by showing your passion and personality, and easy to repeat over and over again. It is helpful if you know it so well that you don't rely on notes and it becomes second nature to you. You are ready to deliver it at a moment's notice.

When you have the right workshop, you attract more people into your sales funnel. When you have the right follow up systems, you move the people who come to your workshop down your sales funnel to become paying clients.

The right workshop is a marketing tool. It will change the way you market your business and get clients.

In this book, you'll find five sections, many helpful suggestions, examples and worksheets meant for you to apply what you're learning to your own workshop.

Part 1: The Foundation. What you'll find here are the five essential steps to deliver workshops that bring in clients. For each step, I describe a common mistake and how to avoid it. I also offer a worksheet with the most essential questions to answer, so you can apply the step to your business. When you can answer all the questions on each worksheet, you're in good shape to create a workshop. You have a solid foundation.

Part 2: The Formula. This part builds on the foundation of Part 1. It is called "The Formula" because it provides a "how-to" guide for the beginning, the middle and the end of your workshop. I also offer a worksheet for each of these sections of your workshop with the most essential questions you'll need to answer. I know how long it takes to design a workshop on your own and I hope that you'll save time with this formula.

When you have designed and developed your workshop on a solid foundation (Part 1 of this book) and followed the formula for the beginning, the middle and the end of your workshop (Part 2 of this book), then you're ready to start marketing it.

Part 3: The Marketing. The marketing of a workshop can be as simple or difficult as you make it. In this part, I recommend a template for your marketing materials, and offer advice on the easiest way to fill your workshop, especially in an urban setting. And, since it comes up so often, I also chime in on the debate to charge or not charge for your workshop.

Part 4: The Delivery. The successful delivery of your workshop depends on many factors. Your social skills matter. So do your facilitation and training skills and how you prepare yourself mentally and emotionally beforehand. In this part, I recommend how to get all these factors right.

Part 5: The Conversion. The point of all this is really to convert your workshop participants into paying clients, right? In this part of the book, I show you how to follow up with your prospects immediately after the workshop, and how to manage a no hype / no pressure conversation with your prospects to close the sale.

When you have mastered the methodology in this book, you will experience the value of having the right workshop as a marketing tool for your business. Even better, you will have new clients and with those new clients, have the opportunity to do even more good in the world!

PART 1:
THE FOUNDATION

In this part of the book, I will teach you the five essential steps to deliver workshops that bring in clients. If you don't build this foundation first, your workshop is not likely to serve as an effective marketing tool for you. It may be fun to deliver, and you may get positive feedback about it, but it may not actually convert your audience into paying clients.

These five steps are a mixture of marketing principles and reminders about human nature and what sells. Although many coaches, consultants and entre-preneurs apply marketing principles to their business, when it comes to developing a presentation or workshop, they forget all about them. They get so excited about the content they want to share and how they will share it that they don't connect their workshop directly to their business and --even more importantly-- to their clients.

Don't let this happen to you! You have valuable skills and could genuinely help people, if only they knew about you and your products or services. The right workshop can serve you for many years, as long as it is built on these five steps, that I call the foundation.

Step #1: Get Clear and Be Specific About the Product or Service You Sell

Have you ever said, "I adapt my services to what my clients need." or "I offer something different for every client?" You may be trying to convey that you are an accommodating person hoping it will catch those potential buyers who may be skeptical that you are the right fit for them. If this describes you, you may be sabotaging the success of your workshop or presentation. Instead of giving a first impression that you're accommodating, you may seem vague and possibly inexperienced at what you do.

Your ideal clients have specific problems and struggles, things that keep them up at night, pains and embarrassments that haunt them over and over. I'm not just talking about some inconvenience that would be nice to avoid, I'm talking about something big that drives them CRAZY! Every time this monster struggle shows up, they get frustrated and fed up and often quit too soon. Doesn't that happen to you sometimes? It definitely happens to me! It's not fun.

I recommend that you create a specific "package" of what you want to sell people as a result of your presentation or workshop. Describe the problem it solves, all the value that it offers, all the benefits that people will get from it, all the reasons why it's important and timely. While it may not be for everyone, it will catch the attention of the people who need exactly what you are offering.

If you would like to deliver workshops or presentations as a marketing tool to bring in clients, then your job is not to solve that whole problem during the workshop, but to prove to your audience you know their problem intimately and how to solve it, when they hire you. In your workshop, you should reflect their problems back to them so clearly and in so much detail that they have no shadow of doubt that you "get them".

As they hear you describe their problem, they should be nodding their heads and thinking to themselves, "Yep, that's me!" or "She's in my head!"

Use the following worksheet to apply what you just read to your own situation. Since it will require clarity, I suggest you do some physical movement (a few stretches or maybe a short dance) and take in some fresh air before you begin. Your brain will appreciate the extra help!

Worksheet:
The Product or Service You Sell

What product or service do you most want to sell? (in your business, as a result of the workshop) Be super specific. Use plain language, not jargon.

What struggle or problem does your product or service solve?

What are the results that your best clients get (or could get) with this product or service?

Describe "the package" of your product or service. (For example, if you're a coach, you likely sell a number of sessions, not session by session.)

Step #2: Get Clear and Be Specific About Your Ideal Clients

If you're self-employed, then you have every reason to (and no excuse not to) be working with your ideal clients – the ones that you relate to, and will benefit the most from your product and services. Your ideal clients are people who recognize that working with you is a key component to realizing their own success. Ideal clients already know that they need your help (you don't have to convince them of that), are easily identified and contacted, get great results from working with you, happily pay what you're worth, refer other clients to you repeatedly, and, most importantly, are people with whom you really enjoy working!

Let's say that I asked you, "What type of person could I refer to you?" Would you be able to describe that person to me in one minute, and really paint a vivid picture for me that I won't forget? If you've done this well, it's likely that someone in particular will come to mind for me. I am more likely to remember your description and refer that type of person to you later on, too.

If you are vague or general in your description, however, I may get the feeling that you are unsure about who is best suited for your products or services. If this is the case, I would be less likely to think of someone in particular and less likely to refer anyone to you.

For example, many coaches and consultants I meet say that their ideal clients are "looking for transformation." Yes, it's true...as coaches and consultants, we want to evoke big, even transformative changes for our clients. Our role is to see the possibility of a bigger and better future for our clients than they are able to see for themselves. The work of great coaches and consultants is transformative. But, let's be honest... do people really say to themselves at night "I'm looking for transformation?" Probably not. Be able to describe your ideal clients in THEIR words!

Your job is to authentically understand your ideal clients by recognizing and relating to their specific weaknesses and strengths, and as much as possible in between! Really seek to know what it's like for them before you market your products and services to them. Feeling and showing your compassion and empathy for someone else's struggles goes a long way in relating to them on both a professional and a personal level, and lets them know that you are invested in them and their success.

Describe what keeps them up at night, what they stress out about, what happens because they are worried about that and even what their inner critic says. Be able to describe their values and principles, what it would look like, be like, feel like when they achieve the results they really want.

If you don't know what it is like to be them, ask them! Here's how. Find someone you already know or build a relationship with someone who, at least at first glance, seems to fit the profile of your ideal client. Do not market anything or try to sell them anything yet! Simply ask them open-ended and non-judgmental questions like:

- What's it like for you (insert the situation you can help with)? What's easy? What's difficult?

- What stresses you out about (insert the situation you can help with)?

- What would it be like to have (insert the situation you can help with) the way you wanted it?

Then, listen. Really listen to them. Be present and postpone judgment or solution finding. Listen for the emotions and what they don't say, as much as what they do say. Record their answers. Ask more specific questions, clarify as necessary and keep listening. Waiting to find solutions is not wasting time - you're gathering valuable information that will help you identify and work toward meaningful and workable solutions.

After you've listened to many people who you believe are your ideal clients, do some analysis and synthesis:

- What are the commonalities among them?

- What are the majority of them worried about?

- What do many of them already know or assume about the situation you can help with?

- What do many of them NOT already know or assume about the situation you can help with?

- What assumptions are many of them making?

- What emotions are typically present when they talk about the situation you can help with – frustration, sadness, fear, for example?

While it's worth the time and effort to research and understand your ideal clients in this way, don't get stuck believing that you have to work with the SAME people or even a narrow spectrum of clients for the rest of your life. You don't. Successful business owners are constantly making adjustments to relate to, and align themselves with the clients they most want to work with. Your job is to clearly decide who you can and want to help in the next year or two.

Use the following worksheet to apply what you just read to your own situation. Since it will require clarity, I suggest you do some physical movement (a few stretches or maybe a short dance) and take in some fresh air before you begin. Your brain will appreciate the extra help!

Worksheet:
Your Ideal Clients

Who suffers from the struggles or problems that your product or service solves? Be super specific.

Why do they need or want the results your product or service can produce? Get even more specific.

What do your ideal clients already know or realize about your product or service? (of your business, not the workshop)

What do your ideal clients not already know or realize about your product or service? This is the best content of your workshop!

Step #3: Get Clear and Be Specific About the Benefits Of Your Workshop

If you're clear on steps one and two, the benefits of your workshop are easy: people learn that you can help them out of their struggles and problems with the product or service you sell. To get people to that point, however, you first have to get them to show up.

That's an obvious statement, I realize, but it's much easier said than done. I'll cover much of the marketing (or how you get the right people to your workshop) in part 3, but the marketing doesn't just start when your workshop is all finished and it's time to invite people to it. It starts long before that. The marketing actually starts with step one, continues with step two and is definitely essential here in step three.

The title and the description of your workshop must also be clear and specific. Many titles and descriptions of presentations or workshops succumb to cuteness over effectiveness. They may be catchy or even rhyme, but they don't resonate with the right people. They could be applied to any industry, in any environment. Too many times, the description doesn't even include whom the workshop is for, or what they want! That's a huge mistake. As one of my clients says, "It's better to be clear than clever." Maybe your workshop title can be both clear and clever, but if not, I recommend you always default to clear.

Remember that most people don't read much. They may only read the title and the first line of your workshop description, and if they are not immediately captivated, they make a quick decision to move on.

The title of your workshop should include the end

result or benefits that your ideal clients want. This is important. It should be stated in their words, not jargon. For example, the title of my workshop is "Deliver Workshops that Bring in Clients". What if it had been called "Instructional Design for Business Owners"? It is, after all, about instructional design.

Despite the fact that my workshop is about instructional design, that is not what my ideal clients want. They may not even know the term and that's okay. They want to bring in new clients to their business and that's what is important here. My workshop, about instructional design, combined with a lot of marketing principles, shows people how they can design, develop and deliver workshops that generate new clients for their business. Therefore, the succinct and effective title is "Deliver Workshops that Bring in Clients".

The short description of your workshop should effectively convey that you will provide real value and <u>specific</u> benefits to a <u>specific</u> kind of person with a <u>specific</u> problem, leading them toward a <u>specific</u> result they want. When those people read it, they will self-identify with the description, give up other plans and show up for your workshop. That's who you want there...*pre-qualified prospects*.

For example, here's the short description of my workshop:

"By the end of this workshop, coaches, consultants and entrepreneurs who love to train people and struggle to find new clients will be able to apply the five essential steps to design a workshop that effectively demonstrates their product or service, and brings in clients to their business."

Your workshop cannot convey everything that you

offer. It should, however, provide your best prospects real value by learning something they didn't already know. It should also provide them an experience they could not get on their own - from reading your website, for example. It is also meant to provide them a taster of who you are, why you do what you do, and how you can solve their problem or struggle, if they hire you.

Similarly, this book, as a written version of my workshop, cannot convey everything that I offer. Hopefully, however, it teaches you a lot about effectively creating and utilizing workshops that you didn't already know. It also provides you an experience and value that you cannot get from my website, and a much better idea of who I am, why I do what I do, and how I can personally help solve your problem or struggle to find new clients, should you decide to work with me.

Use the following worksheet to apply what you just read to your own situation. Since it will require clarity, I suggest you do some physical movement (a few stretches or maybe a short dance) and take in some fresh air before you begin. Your brain will appreciate the extra help!

Worksheet:
The Benefits Of Your Workshop

Which part of your product or service will your ideal clients get a taste of during your workshop? (This comes from what they <u>do not</u> currently know or realize about your product or service.)

What experience will your ideal clients have at your workshop (about your product or service) that they wouldn't have on their own?

Fill in the following sentence and use it to guide your workshop description:

By the end of this workshop, *(fill in with a description of your ideal clients, including both an easy identifier and a struggle they have)*

_____

_____

will be able to *(fill in with an action verb)*

_____

(fill in something related to your product or service)

_____

that results in *(fill in with the end results or benefits that your ideal clients get from your product / service)*

_____

Create three draft titles that clearly and succinctly state the results your ideal clients want:

1. _____

_____

2. _____

_____

3._____

_____

Step #4: Connect with Your "Why"

Self-employed coaches, consultants and entrepreneurs face all kinds of obstacles – from isolation to self-doubt to financial stress. Being self-employed can be a roller coaster ride. The reality of paying the bills, building the website, finding clients, getting out there, and creating new marketing materials can be overwhelming. Because of the daily stress, you may forget, or unintentionally create distance, from the real reason you want to help.

You have a powerful story to tell. Your job is to find the meaning and the lessons in your own story, to connect (or reconnect) to it, and be able to portray the reason that you do what you do.

The reasons to know your "Why" are to:

- realize your unique value,
- gain recognition for bringing it forward,
- relate with your clients' unique "why",
- know how you fit into a bigger picture,
- communicate it in ways that compel others to listen, pay attention and connect, and
- create valuable alignment between your brand and that of your ideal clients.

In his book and popular Ted Talk called *Start with Why*, Simon Sinek says, "People don't buy what you do, they buy *why* you do it." Let your "Why" be known!

For example, here's the difference between <u>what</u> I do and <u>why</u> I do it.

<u>What I do</u>: I help coaches, consultants and entrepreneurs communicate their skills to, and build relationships with people who need them and will pay for them.

<u>Why I do what I do</u>: I believe that so many coaches, consultants and entrepreneurs have a natural gift for teaching or training others. They have great skills, products and services that the world needs. They could provide a lot of value to the right people, if only those "right people" could find them. I believe they can use this gift or talent to find more prospects, provide an authentic experience of their work and convert their audiences into paying clients. At the same time, I believe that creating workshops is far too much work to <u>not</u> bring in clients from them. It doesn't have to be that way. With the <u>right</u> signature workshop, plenty of preparation, and a lot of justified confidence, a workshop can be a rewarding way to grow and shape a successful business.

If you're not quite ready to articulate why you do what you do and you're thinking, "I do it for the money," I challenge that sentiment. There are an infinite number of things that you could do if it were just for the money. There is some reason that you choose to do what you do. If you'd like to start attracting your ideal clients, it may be the right time to gain this self-awareness.

If you're curious to figure out your "Why" and you like to self-reflect through writing, I recommend the book by Pamela Slim called *Body of Work: Finding the Thread that Ties Your Story Together*. She teaches how to find the patterns and the lessons of life, with all its complexities, and how it is relevant, and, in fact, the cause of who we are and what we do. She also has a free workbook including exercises filled with questions that guide us through some deeply important self-reflection.

If you're not the type to read that book and complete the workbook on your own, then I recommend that you consider hiring a qualified life coach: someone who is extremely thoughtful and insightful. Someone who listens for the patterns, trends, and recurring themes and is genuinely curious about what they mean. Ask this coach to either help you complete the workbook together or, in his or her own way, to help you realize the story behind your own body of work, and the specific "Why" of your work.

Likewise, if you're also not the type to thoroughly read this book, apply its principles, and complete the worksheets on your own, then I recommend you consider one of my programs. In my programs, you will receive individualized attention and specific guidance that applies directly to your situation, your business and is aligned with your "Why". People who successfully complete my programs have a signature presentation or workshop that they are confident delivering and plays a pivotal role in attracting clients to their business.

Use the following worksheet to apply what you just read to your own situation. Since it will require clarity, I suggest you do some physical movement (a few stretches or maybe a short dance) and take in some fresh air before you begin. Your brain will appreciate the extra help!

Worksheet:
Connect With Your "Why"

Why do you do what you do?

Why do you do it in the way that you do?

"I believe…. (finish the sentence) or, "I believe my ideal clients (with my help) can…(finish the sentence)."

Step #5: Let Your Passion and Personality Shine Through

You may be asking, "What does my passion or personality have to do with my workshop?" or "I don't have time to include that, and besides, people don't care."

You may also be thinking: "I like that.", "Good analogy!" "I wish I could be more like her." "I'm impressed!", or even "That's weird." or "I'm skeptical." We are all absorbing impressions of each other and everything all the time. In Malcolm Gladwell's book, *Blink*, he describes how we often have an intuitive hit about something or someone right away. This can happen literally in the blink of an eye. We may be most aware of our first impressions of people, but we accumulate impressions of people, places and things every time we encounter them.

If, at your workshops, you're trying to appear more one way, or less another way, you are likely not showing up with the level of authenticity and self-confidence that sells. If you don't let your passion and personality shine through, frankly, you just blend in. You don't shine. A few months after your workshop, the audience may not remember you or your name. Your first impression may not have been effective enough.

As you design, develop and deliver your workshop, be YOU.

For example, here's a little about my passion and personality and how I use it to improve my workshop. I love to dance, stretch, and do yoga. I'm not (and never have been) a professional dancer or yogi, but they've been lifelong loves of mine. I dance every week. I regularly go to dance performances, dance classes and weekend dance workshops. I read books about dance, I buy fun clothes to dance in, and many of my closest friends are also dancers. I also stretch and do yoga frequently. In fact, I'm somewhat known for stretching in odd places, like airports, parties, standing in line, and yes, you guessed it, even at my workshops.

At the beginning of my workshop and during the breaks throughout it, I invite the participants to dance or stretch with me. For example, when I delivered my signature workshop at The Power Conference in front of 75 people, I had music playing in the room as people were arriving. I invited them to put their things down and join me in some playful dancing –free form– without any instruction. At the session start time, I turned off the music, and was formally introduced by the conference organizer. The whole room was smiling and engaged.

If you've ever done public speaking, you know that the energy or mood of the audience makes a big difference. That said, you may feel as if you don't have any control over how people show up – what mood they are in, or what their attitude is. Not true. You do.

I create the energy I want at my workshops – fun and light-hearted, yet also productive. I do that by sharing my passion. If possible and/or appropriate, I recommend you try to find a creative and productive way to do the same.

Similarly, share your positive personality traits that are most accessible to you. Don't cover up or change who you are. Talk like you would normally talk. Don't get fancy or too formal, or too "professional." Show up wearing what you would wear if you were already working with your ideal clients. The first impression that you make may not appeal to everyone, and that's okay. You'll appeal to your own tribe - the people who respect and admire you for who you are, and how you can help them.

As a personal example, I used to try to dress like my audience and impress them with my word choices. At that time, I was working in Latin America, so I wore a lot of black business suits and high heels and I used big words to sound ten years older and show off my fluency in Spanish. While I don't know if I fooled any-one, I definitely didn't feel relaxed or authentic. Today, I wear the creative clothes I feel most comfortable in, and talk like I normally and naturally talk – in English or in Spanish.

I'll cover this topic in much more detail in Part 4: The Delivery.

Use the following worksheet to apply what you just read to your own situation. Since it will require clarity, I suggest you do some physical movement (a few stretches or maybe a short dance) and take in some fresh air before you begin. Your brain will appreciate the extra help!

Worksheet:
Let Your Passion and Personality Shine Through

What do your ideal clients appreciate about who you are?

Which elements of your passion and personality do you show with your most supportive and compassionate family, friends, spouse, life partner, or life coach?

How could you show your most authentic self (including your passion and personality) in your workshop?

PART 2:
THE FORMULA

It's easiest to design your workshop when you already know how long it will be. I've seen people begin to create their workshop without a clear sense of this, and usually what happens is that the workshop becomes longer and longer. They have not needed to edit their work, and so they end up including many (maybe all?) of the good ideas they have. Often, once they know how much time they will have for their workshop, they have to go back and cut much of it out. At that point, they have developed a certain attachment to what is included and have a harder time editing it.

If you're not sure yet how long your workshop will be, then I suggest that you skip to part 3 of this book and think about the marketing of your workshop before you begin designing it. Doing some marketing research, will help you to decide on the length of your workshop. When you come back to part 2 to design it, you'll avoid that scenario I described above.

If, however, you do know how long your workshop will

be, now it's time to do some simple math. A workshop that is designed to bring in clients should have three equally important parts: the beginning, the middle and the end. I have found that most people are best at the middle, and they neglect to focus on a proper beginning and end. Sometimes, their entire workshop is what I would consider the middle.

Don't ignore all the opportunity that lies in the beginning and the end of your workshop. They have specific and very important jobs to do and, together, they should account for about one-third of your workshop time. For example, for a 90-minute workshop, divide it into three parts, this way:

15 minutes	=	beginning
+ 1 hour	=	middle
+ 15 minutes	=	end
1.5 hour	=	total workshop time

Within the times you allocate for the beginning, middle and end, here's the formula for what to do and how to do it.

The Beginning of Your Workshop

Generally at the beginning of a workshop, we're used to two things: hearing the background and credentials of the person presenting and some type of icebreaker or activity for everyone to introduce themselves to each other. When you design a workshop that is designed to bring in clients, neither of those may be needed. I'm not saying they are bad to do, but the question is do they really bring the most value possible to your ideal clients? Remember, that is the goal.

Besides, if someone will introduce you to the audience before you begin your workshop, then they can list your degrees, talents, and previous jobs, if they prefer that. If you can, however, write the script for the person who will introduce you, so that it's compelling and specifically describes the accomplishments that speak to solving the struggles of your ideal clients. If you're not sure what your ideal clients struggle with, then I recommend you re-read step two of Part 1 of this book: The Foundation.

As the presenter or trainer of the workshop, describing your background and listing your credentials may seem like the right thing to do, and I hear people say *"don't I have to tell them about me first?"* Well, I don't mean to be insensitive, but it's not about you, it's about them!

Your audience cares about why they came to and what they want from your workshop. Instead, you can use the beginning of your workshop to earn credibility, and they will get to know you in the process. You easily earn credibility by showing your ideal clients that you really understand them – that you know what it's like to be in their shoes. You remind them of their struggles and provide reassurance that you can help them. Be as specific and detailed as possible. Get inside their head and their emotions! Say what their self-critic says –as if you are their inner voice. Describe the ways in which they waste time, or get stuck or sabotage their own success.

For example, here's mine, in plain language:

"You know how, when you put so much time into preparing your workshop and then you don't get clients out of it? This means that you've spent a lot of time (likely unpaid time) that provides no return on investment, which leads to disappointment and even frustration."

But don't just leave them there hanging high and dry!

Show your ideal clients what it will be like when they solve their problems and struggles. Again, be as specific and detailed as possible. Describe their dreams and aspirations back to them – even what they might do with their free time, or their new found confidence, or security or money, whatever it is! If you don't already know this about your ideal clients, simply ask them! Don't make this too complicated.

For example, here's mine:

"It doesn't have to be this way! If you are passionate about helping people and are a strong communicator, with a product or service that the world needs, you could provide a lot of value to the right people, if only those "right people" could find you. I believe you can find prospects, provide them an authentic experience of your work and convert them into paying clients. With my proven methodology, plenty of preparation, and a lot of justified confidence, the right signature workshop can be a rewarding way to

bring in clients and grow your business. And, that's why I do what I do."

This is your chance to share your "I believe" statement or your "Why". If your "Why" is aligned with your work, then likely, seeing your ideal clients free of those problems and living a better future is part of it. Now when you share that with them, it likely resonates more deeply with them, making you more likable and giving your ideal clients more reasons to trust you and feel aligned with you. People who like you, trust you and feel aligned with you are much more likely to hire you, and that's the intention of your workshop – to find and align yourself with prospects who are likely to hire you. Align yourself with both your ideal clients' problems and the solutions that will change their current situation, and ultimately their life.

Use the following worksheet to apply what you just read to your own situation. Since it will require clarity, I suggest you do some physical movement (a few stretches or maybe a short dance) and take in some fresh air before you begin. Your brain will appreciate the extra help!

✒ Worksheet:
The Beginning of Your Workshop

Here are the steps for the beginning of your workshop, in my preferred order, which has proven effective for me and my clients.

Reflect back the problems and struggles of your most ideal client. What are they?

You might want to use this formula: "You know how when you _____? This means that _____, which leads to _____.

Describe the desired future of your most ideal client, free of those problems and struggles. What does that look like? This could be the greatest success story of your best client. Describe it as the story of ONE specific person or organization, not a group of clients.

Provide reassurance that you (with your product or service) can help your ideal client achieve that desired future or greatest success story. How will you assure them?

Convey and demonstrate your "why" or "I believe" statement. What is yours?

The Middle of Your Workshop

The middle of your workshop is when you provide experiences that demonstrate the salient points (or most needed aspects) of your service or product and how your ideal clients could get the results they want. You will refer back to these salient points in group discussions, at the end of your workshop, and in your follow-up. In other words, whatever you choose as the focus of your workshop will inform how you will close the sale, by converting your audience into clients. This is a very important decision – get feedback and take your time to develop the specific points you want your ideal clients to remember and take with them.

Two common mistakes I frequently see when people design the middle of their workshop are:

1) Failure to focus on relevant and substantive workshop experiences. I've seen people include experiences in their workshops that don't <u>directly relate to the service or product they offer</u>. They include an experiential activity, and people may enjoy it, but it doesn't provide the value that their ideal clients came to the workshop for because it doesn't easily translate into or enhance the substance of the workshop. Instead, I recommend you scrutinize every experience or salient point you consider with the question: "Does this directly help my ideal clients overcome their obstacles?" If not, consider a more applicable experience or explicitly connect the experience to the substance of the workshop. After all, that's why people are at your workshop.

Still not sure what that could be? Here's a tip. **The experience should be about what they do not know or realize about how to achieve the results that they want.**

2) Too much breadth and not enough depth. People often include too many experiences for the amount of time they have. They only allow a superficial look at a topic, when there is usually so much more richness and understanding to tease out of it. This often happens when they fall into the trap of giving out handouts, worksheets or resource lists without the context to make them useful or the time to allow for learning. Instead, I recommend you make the hard choice of providing only what is absolutely most valuable for them. You can share the rest as part of your Follow-Up Free Opt-In or marketing strategy. I'll cover both of those concepts in Part 5 of this book. Keep reading!

In the middle section of your workshop, I recommend you accommodate different learning styles and create an active and safe learning environment. You should vary your methods frequently to hold people's attention. Your methods should be experiential, so your audience actively participates. Whenever the participants are just sitting and listening to you is the part that they are most likely to forget.

Maybe you've already seen these statistics, published originally by the psychiatrist, William Glasser, but a reminder never hurts. We remember:

- 10% of what we read
- 20% of what we hear
- 30% of what we see
- 50% of what we see and hear
- 70% of what we discuss with others
- 80% of what we personally experience
- 95% of what we teach others

With this in mind, I recommend you create a workshop in which you provide the opportunity for people to discuss with others, experience what you are proposing, and share their own knowledge by teaching one another during the workshop.

Another one of your jobs as the leader of your workshop is to effectively "process" the experiences that you create. To "process" means to allow for and to cultivate discussion and learning. There are specific ways to lead people through an experience so that they get the most effective learning and value possible.

The standard and most beloved method used in the training and development field is Kolb's Experiential Learning Cycle, and is described like this: Effective learning is seen when a person progresses through a cycle of four stages: of *(1) having a concrete experience followed by (2) observation of and reflection on that experience which leads to (3) the formation of abstract concepts (analysis) and generalizations (conclusions) which are then (4) used to test hypothesis in future situations which result in new experiences.*

If you are already an experienced trainer or facilitator, then this is merely a refresher. If this concept is new to you, then take advantage of the next worksheet to guide you through it and provide the processing questions that skilled trainers and facilitators ask.

During the middle of your workshop, you have the opportunity to highlight examples, so that the participants understand more about your product or service. You can provide examples of your own experience, but it can be more powerful to provide examples (or relate stories) about the experiences of your clients.

If you don't already have client success stories, don't let

that stop you. Describe the changes you've influenced and inspired along the way. For example, when I was just starting out, before any of my clients had achieved getting new clients from their workshop, I said this, to demonstrate my value:

"One of my clients was going to networking events looking for people to attend her workshop. She met many people, and even though she invited them to her workshop, very few of them would show up. Her marketing efforts were not working, which meant that she was frustrated and, unfortunately, her business wasn't growing. After I helped her get clear and specific about her service and her ideal clients, I recommended that she try networking at different events, where there was a higher concentration of her ideal clients. And, instead of marketing her workshop right away, I suggested that she use that opportunity to do more research about her ideal clients and what results they were most looking for. She followed my advice, and gathered invaluable information about her ideal clients. Now she has ditched her previous workshop and feels more confident to design the right workshop."

In that example, I don't claim that this client had delivered her workshop or brought in new clients yet. That's because she hadn't. She had only begun to work with me, and she was one of my very first clients. I had only begun to help people deliver workshops that bring in clients. While I was adding value, I couldn't yet claim that my clients had achieved the end results they ultimately wanted – new clients. That said, I still articulated an example at my workshop of the value that I provided up until that point, being honest, and not exaggerating the truth.

We all have to start somewhere. Be honest with yourself, and start where YOU are!

Not sure how you add value? I see that a lot.

Sometimes it's hard to recognize your own value, especially when you have not yet realized your full potential or you're too close to it. Sometimes, my clients undermine themselves and their value and say things like "Doesn't everyone already know that?"

The short answer is no. I was taught a helpful concept that I'll share with you.

Help others with what comes naturally and seems absolutely obvious to you. It's not natural or obvious to others.

Something is only easy when you know it, have practiced it, shared it, repeated it, and mastered it. While you were mastering something, others were mastering their own thing.

For example, speaking Spanish comes naturally to me. I learned it as a child, I majored in it in college, and my work - for ten years - was entirely in Spanish. I wrote training manuals in Spanish, I delivered workshops in Spanish and I found it easy. Yet, I know that learning a foreign language is really difficult for others.

While I was busy mastering Spanish, some of my friends were learning to sing and play musical instruments – something I find incredibly difficult and would love to learn. Playing their instrument and singing beautifully is natural to them now, but it is far from natural or obvious to me!

Again, just because something is easy for you now, doesn't mean it is easy for others! I realize that I'm stating the obvious, but I bring it up, because I witness people suffering from doubt and self-sabotaging thoughts about the value of their product or service. They sometimes get stuck at this point, and I hope to prevent that from happening to you.

If you have any doubt about this, please find the people who you believe might be looking for the results you can help them achieve. Ask them if they want those results, or if they know anyone else who does. Don't try to sell them anything yet, just gather information and seek to learn the value of your product or service.

If, after doing that, you're still stuck, it may be worth investing in a program like mine designed to specifically help you. With the right individualized attention, you will discover what comes naturally and seems obvious to you about your own product or service, but isn't obvious to others. That knowledge in and of itself is a gift to yourself and your business. You and your business are worth the investment.

Now, a word of caution.

If you are a public speaker, or have a natural talent for communicating or facilitating groups, you may find it easier to deliver your workshop than it is for people without that experience or talent. For you, I offer this word of caution! Please don't rely solely on that skill or experience. It helps, for sure, but it's not –ultimately- what causes people to convert into clients.

Converting attendees into clients, generally speaking, requires three things:

1. They *know you* (who you really are, not just your name);

2. They *like you* (what you believe and why you do what you do), and

3. They *trust you* and believe you can help them with exactly what they need.

These three things must be conveyed convincingly in your signature workshop. Even if you are already a public speaker or strong communicator, to successfully convey these three essential factors, your workshop should still be built on a solid foundation, as described in Part 1 of this book.

Use the following worksheet to apply what you just read to your own situation. Since it will require clarity, I suggest you do some physical movement (a few stretches or maybe a short dance) and take in some fresh air before you begin. Your brain will appreciate the extra help!

Worksheet:
The Middle of Your Workshop

Here are the steps for the middle of your workshop, in my proven and preferred order.

Determine the most salient points (or needed aspects) of your product or service for your ideal clients. What will those be?

Create an experience to actively engage your ideal clients in the most salient points (or needed aspects) of your product or service. What will the experience be?

Ensure that the experience relates directly to the results that your ideal clients want. How does the experience contribute to those results? Refer back to Part 1: The Foundation to refresh your memory about the results that your ideal clients want.

Allow the participants to observe and reflect on that experience. How will you do this? Skilled trainers and facilitators ask an open-ended question such as, "What did you observe?" or "What happened?"

Encourage the participants to analyze and draw conclusions about that experience. How will you do this? Skilled trainers and facilitators ask an open-ended question such as, "What does that mean for you?" or "Why does that matter?"

Encourage the participants to use their new learning in future situations for new experiences and outcomes. How will you do this? Skilled trainers and facilitators ask an open-ended question such as, "Now what?" or "How will you apply this to your own situation?"

The End of Your Workshop

I'll be perfectly frank with you. The end of a workshop is what most people mess up. If you want to bring clients into your business, be extra careful here.

By marketing your workshop, you have already created some awareness about you and the product or service you sell. This means that whoever has seen your marketing materials is at the top of your sales funnel.

The people who have shown up for your workshop have already expressed an interest. Whether they paid for your workshop or not, they gave their time and that is an extremely important step, especially in today's busy world with lots of opportunities and demands for our time. At your invitation, they have moved themselves down your sales funnel, showing interest and engagement.

During the middle of your workshop, they have become more informed and gained a much better understanding of you, and the product or service you sell. The end of your workshop is when you explain how you know that your product or service works, address any resistance and describe the action you want your ideal clients to take.

Explain how you know that your product or service works

If you've followed your own advice and have achieved impressive results with your own product or service, then describe your current reality. If possible, it's even better to describe the current reality of the clients you've helped achieve their desired future with the product or service you offer. The ideal prospects among your workshop participants will likely resonate with these stories.

You can and should convey the success of your previous clients by sharing their testimonials during your workshop. Their testimonials should speak to the <u>results</u> of your work, <u>not the process</u>. They are most effective when they include pictures, first and last names and any kind of descriptor, such as company name or title.

Address any resistance

Once you have explained how you know that your product or service works, it's possible that some of the workshop participants will still be skeptical that it could actually help them. They may put up resistance, even if only in their thoughts and don't express it. This is your opportunity to address it.

I suggest you demonstrate that you understand how your ideal clients will offer resistance or sabotage themselves. This is not for the direct purpose of convincing them to do anything, but rather to remind them of the cost or lost opportunity if they don't engage with your product or service. Again, you are not directly trying to convince them to become a client, you are pointing out the truth of what often happens to people who sabotage themselves by not taking advantage of a product or service they need.

For example, here's the resistance I see and how I address it.

"You may be thinking to yourself that you've learned enough about workshops to create your own signature workshop that brings in clients. You may also be saying to

yourself that you'll create your workshop on your own and see if you get new clients from it first, then decide if you need my help. I understand this way of thinking. I tend to be a "DIY'er" myself.

The truth is that designing, developing and delivering your workshop takes an incredible amount of time and effort, especially if you are not 100% clear about the foundation of your workshop. Instructional designers have equations for calculating how much time it takes, and some say it takes 70-100 hours of prep time for every 1 hour of delivery time.

I've seen people try to design their workshop on their own, and while they may have fun delivering it, unfortunately, it doesn't achieve their goal to bring in clients. That's disappointing to them and their ideal prospects have still not found the help they need. Unfortunately, some of them continue to re-design their workshop over and over. Imagine how much time that takes!

If you're going to invest the (unpaid) time and energy to create your own workshop, I suggest that you spend that time wisely and use the various resources available to you to create the right signature workshop that converts your audience into clients."

Describe the action you want your ideal clients to take

After you've addressed the resistance in people's minds, this is when you offer a clear, inviting and easy next step, sometimes called a "call to action".

If you are practiced at "selling from the stage" then you may feel confident asking the participants to buy right then and there. This is sometimes called "making an offer." Many people who sell from the stage provide a discount, or extra bonus, that makes their offer even more attractive to act upon immediately.

First, a word of caution about doing this. You want to describe the <u>results</u> that people get with your product or service. Please don't fall into the trap of describing the <u>process</u> of how they will get there. As the well-known sales coach, Lisa Sasevich, says "Regarding your offer, remember; they're buying the destination, not the plane!"

If, however, you are not confident selling from the stage yet, or if that's not appropriate for the situation where you're presenting (many conferences don't allow it), there are alternatives. In that case, I suggest that you offer an incentive for people to stay connected to you. This incentive is something that you give people for free, in exchange for their contact information and their permission to use it.

Provide your audience a good reason to hear from you again. This good reason can be something free, and of high value, that they need and want in that moment. I'll call this something that is free and of high value, the "Follow-Up Free Opt-In." When people accept it, they move further down your sales funnel and become one step closer to a client.

The "Follow-Up Free Opt-In" serves three purposes:

1. You have a reason to invite them to "opt-in," which means they give you permission to be in touch with them, and they move down your sales funnel once again.

2. You have a reason to be in touch with them

again and they are expecting to hear from you – even <u>waiting</u> to hear from you; and

3. You continue to provide them real value, which means they get more benefits from you, even after your workshop. The ideal clients among the audience will consider it timely too, since they will be ready for it.

I recommend that you do <u>not</u> provide the "Follow-Up Free Opt-In" directly at the workshop itself. Rather, at the end of your workshop, you <u>describe the value and benefits</u> that people will get from it and <u>how</u> they can get it.

Your "Follow-Up Free Opt-In" should not be a surprise or new concept. It should be a very logical and extremely helpful extension of what you've already covered in the workshop.

For example, in my signature workshop, I only cover Part 1 of this book. My "Follow-Up Free Opt-In" is very similar to Part 2 of this book.

Developing an effective "Follow-Up Free Opt-In" is a bit of an art and a science. If you know your material and what your ideal clients need, developing the opt-in may take some time, but is within your ability to create. If you are having a difficult time determining what to provide, start paying attention to what your ideal clients ask you during or after your workshop, including any post workshop correspondence with potential clients. They will often tell you what they need or want.

If you're still unsure of what your "Follow-Up Free Opt-In" could be, the right individualized attention, like the services I provide to my clients, could help you discover what your ideal clients want so badly that they are eagerly waiting for you to provide it for them. The understanding of what is <u>that</u> valuable to your ideal clients is yet another level of clarity for you, and another boost for your business. It's worth knowing.

Now, here is where you can prepare yourself to make the conversion process easier. Although you'll read a lot more about this in Part 5: The Conversion, the end of your workshop is the most important opportunity for you to begin a longer term relationship with the participants of your workshop.

I recommend that you set up the "Follow-Up Free Opt-In" to be in exchange for their business card or complete contact information. By "complete," I recommend that you ask for their full name, business name, website, email address, phone number, and if possible, even their physical address.

When you have their complete contact information, you are able to keep in touch with them in a variety of ways. The "Follow-Up Free Opt-In" will be among the first things they receive from you, after the workshop, but, here's the catch. It cannot be the last thing they hear from you! Far from it, in fact.

It's likely that your workshop participants are not ready for your product or service in the very moment that they meet you or come to your workshop, but they anticipate needing it in the future. Your job is to stay fresh on their mind, so they don't forget you and your product or service.

So many people who offer workshops don't follow-up, or follow-through or stay in touch with workshop participants over time. This is a necessary ingredient for converting your audience into paying clients. I recommend you continue to offer more value to your workshop participants on a consistent basis, specifically on the product or service you described during your workshop.

Many coaches, consultants and entrepreneurs offer to send people their newsletter, if they have one. While news of your business growth, and your future workshops may be interesting to some of them, it also may <u>not</u> be enough value for others.

This is when your knowledge of your ideal clients becomes critical again. If you took the time to dive deeply into Part 1 of this book, then you likely under-stand what is most appealing and valuable to your ideal clients. If you didn't study Part 1 of this book, then I recommend you go back and do that now. The thinking you do in Part 1 informs your decisions for Part 2.

When you know what is most appealing and valuable to your clients, I recommend that you provide <u>that</u> to your workshop participants over time, in small, timely doses. Remember, if you're not sure what they need, ask them!

Sweeten the deal

After you've described the action that you want your ideal clients to take, now you can provide an even sweeter incentive so your ideal clients elect to move even further down your sales funnel. This may be easiest to do while they are most engaged with you – at your workshop!

I recommend that you think carefully about what this will be. Many of my clients assume that the best incentive is a discount in price. This may or may not be the sweetest deal for your ideal clients. Again, ask them what would be the sweetest deal you could offer them. Let them tell you what they want and need.

Use the following worksheet to apply what you just read to your own situation. Since it will require clarity, I suggest you do some physical movement (a few stretches or maybe a short dance) and take in some fresh air before you begin. Your brain will appreciate the extra help!

Worksheet:
The End of Your Workshop

Here are the steps for the end of your workshop. I suggest following them in this order:

Explain how you know that your solution, (your product or service) works. What will you say?

Insert a few testimonials. Which client testimonials will you share?

Address any resistance that your ideal clients have and the impact of it. What resistance and what impact will you describe?

What is your "Follow-Up Free Opt-In"? Give it a title and describe the benefits it provides.

Describe the action you want your ideal clients to take. What action will you suggest?

Sweeten the deal. What incentive will you offer?

How will you keep in touch with the workshop participants over time?

PART 3:
THE MARKETING

How to Create Marketing Materials for Your Workshop

Ever wondered if you need printed materials or if electronic marketing materials will be enough? It all comes back to knowing your ideal clients. When do they most acutely experience the pain that you help them with? Where are they? Are they in their office? Their home? The gym? The grocery store? Where do they convene? What do they read?

I recommend that you place the marketing materials where they will most frequently and most easily see them, based on their habits and routines.

Here's a checklist for your marketing materials, in either printed or electronic form:

- Title (see step three of Part 1: The Foundation)
- Description (see step three of Part 1: The Foundation)

- Client Testimonial
- Short description of you
- Great picture of you
- Date, Time, Location of your workshop
- Price
- Contact information

Looks matter, and brevity is your friend. Remember a few basics:

- A great picture does get attention and can go a long way.
- People do judge a book by its cover. The design of your marketing materials conveys an impression of you, your product or service, and your business. Make it count.
- People don't read much. They scan the headlines and make very quick decisions to keep reading or move on.
- A glowing testimonial of you, your workshop or your product or service can also help.

The Easiest Way to Fill Your Workshop

The challenges of marketing become very obvious when you try to self-produce and self-promote your own workshop. If you've ever tried marketing your own workshop, you know how much time and effort it takes. Depending on where you live, how unique your product or service is in your region, and how much of a following you have, you may find marketing your workshop to be easier or harder. If there are many people who do something similar to what you do, it could make the marketing more difficult. If you live in a region with a lot of entrepreneurs and a lot of workshops, this could make it challenging. If you don't have a pre-qualified list of subscribers or huge number of social media followers that are waiting for your workshop, this could also make the marketing harder. For all these reasons, I'm sharing some of the easiest ways to fill your presentation or workshop with the right people.

Of course, social media can spread the news about your workshop far and wide, faster and easier than most other means, but it may not be the most effective method. For example, I recently searched EventBrite (the commonly used web-based invitation software) for events happening from Tuesday through Saturday in the Washington, DC area. Much to my surprise, there were 1,613 events, on 135 different pages within a 20-mile radius. Hard to stand out? Yes!

What I suggest instead, is that you partner with groups that already convene and communicate with your ideal clients and ask them to produce (and market) your workshop for you. This emphasizes the need to identify and know your ideal clients well, so you can find the groups that they already belong to, or the places where they already spend time and money.

You can volunteer to be a guest speaker at one of these venues, groups or associations, or as part of their programming. For example, if a local group of people who are similar to your ideal clients has regular monthly evening programs, then you can offer to contribute, by offering your workshop for one of them.

If you're just getting started, it may be best to adopt your workshop to the length of the typical events of these groups. You want to make it as easy as possible for them to say yes to you and your workshop. If and when you have a strong relationship with these groups, they might produce an event accommodating your preferred dates, time of day and the length of your workshop at a later date. In the beginning, however, I recommend that you fit into their schedule and their routine. You are, after all, a guest.

Established groups already have a communication channel that likely reaches a wider audience than yours. They are able to reach their followers or subscribers that you don't already know, and that don't already know you. Take advantage of that opportunity.

At the same time, don't leave the whole burden of marketing your workshop to your hosts. Help them to help you! You will want to provide your hosts with the title and description of your workshop, a short bio and great picture of yourself.

Unfortunately, however, sometimes hosts don't necessarily know how or may not make the time to effectively promote your workshop. Although this may not be an ideal host for you, if you're starting out and it's your only option, don't let this stop you. Here are some suggestions to discuss with them ahead of time:

1. Set the date for two months in the future. While some people may not pay attention to dates that are that far in advance, it will catch the attention of your most ideal clients. When the title and description of your workshop truly resonates with them, they will save the date. They may even cancel other plans to be there.

2. Promote your workshop as soon as possible, and frequently. Promotion should include some type of registration process so you can check the progress and plan your promotion accordingly. If your workshop is strictly a

drop-in and no type of pre-registration is encouraged, then you are setting yourself up for a possible disappointment.

3. Use as many delivery channels as possible to promote the workshop: Eventbrite, Facebook, Twitter, Instagram, LinkedIn, blog posts, newsletters, event calendars, printed flyers, post-cards, word-of-mouth, networking and more.

4. When you (or your host) introduce yourself in person, be sure to mention an extremely short (about 20 seconds) description of the workshop and the date of it.

5. Check with your workshop host to ensure that marketing efforts are going smoothly. Ask about what promotion is completed, who it has reached, registration numbers, and the data that proves that your ideal clients are seeing the promotion of the workshop.

6. If necessary, increase the frequency of the promotional efforts in the week to ten days before your workshop. Many people are so busy and have so many options for professional and personal development that they make a decision to attend at the last minute.

7. Send a reminder to the registered participants, preferably three days and one day before your workshop. Include any logistical information such as transportation, parking, entrance codes, and if snacks or drinks will be provided.

Even if your host promotes your workshop for you, you should still also promote your own workshop. This gives you an opportunity to cross-promote their venue or group, too. If you already have social media followers or subscribers, then logically you would tell them about your workshop, always making it as easy as possible for them to find the information.

If you don't yet have followers or subscribers in your own list or on social media, then you may also want to ask well-connected people in your network to help you get the word out.

The more personal your request, the more likely your connections will be able to help you. A quick phone conversation to ask them for this favor may be more effective than a group email request, for example. To make it even easier for them, you can send them your workshop marketing material and sample social media posts.

Use the following worksheet to apply what you just read to your own situation. Since it will require clarity, I suggest you do some physical movement (a few stretches or maybe a short dance) and take in some fresh air before you begin. Your brain will appreciate the extra help!

Worksheet:
Where to Market Your Workshop

Where do your ideal clients network or convene?

Who do they already hire to provide other products and services to them?

What groups are they in?

What conferences do they attend?

What associations do they belong to?

The Debate About Whether to Charge or Not

Should you charge for a workshop? It is easy to get excited about a one-to-many model, in which you make money from your workshop as an income stream for your business. However, let's review the purpose of your workshop.

The purpose of your signature workshop is to market yourself and your business, by finding your ideal clients, providing them value and winning their respect.

With clarity about the purpose of your signature workshop, you have some strategic decisions to make. Here are some reasons to charge or not charge for your workshop. I don't really take a side, but rather, I recommend that you consider your own current situation as you make this decision.

Ensuring that your workshop is attended and creates traction for your business is, for some, the hardest part. If you are creating a new workshop or are entering a new market with your workshop, be careful that you are not making your decision to charge or not based on the situation you hope to have in one year, but rather, your reality at the moment. You can always change your mind and charge more or less, but here are some considerations if you're just starting out.

If you charge for your workshop:

- You may find that the people who show up have pre-qualified themselves. They have already identified their need for what you offer and showed a willingness to give you their money, which is a positive sign.

- Some people are more likely to show up for something that they have already paid for.

- You may not attract as many people who are willing to pre-pay for a workshop when they are used to attending them for free.

- You may exclude people who are especially tight on finances at the moment. Remember, people's financial situations change.

If you do not charge for your workshop:

- You may find that more people come, but it's possible they are not as pre-qualified or interested in what you offer since they didn't have to spend anything to find out.

- Although they may RSVP, some people do not necessarily show up for events that don't require any pre-payment.

- You may attract people whose finances are tight at the moment, so they are unable to pay you what you're worth right away. Again, remember, people's financial situations change.

Your decision comes down to knowing your audience, how much time and disposable income they have and what they are used to. It also depends on where you live, how unique your product or service is in your region, and how much of a following you have. If your area is full of people who do something similar to what you do, or you don't have a subscriber list of pre-qualified prospects to invite, then not charging for your workshop may be a good solution in the beginning, to get plenty of practice delivering it, and create a reputation.

Remember that the purpose of your workshop is to market yourself. It's easier to justify not charging when you consider your workshop the marketing tool that it is, rather than a source of income itself. Many businesses don't <u>make</u> money on their marketing, they need to <u>spend</u> some, instead. You might need to also.

PART 4:
THE DELIVERY

Are you practiced at managing group dynamics? Do you know how to read a group's energy? Do you know how adults learn best? Are you ready for a nay-saying participant?

When you can confidently answer yes to these questions, you'll likely be at ease in front of a new group. You already know that you can handle almost any situation with grace and ease. This will help you stay calm while preparing and delivering your workshop.

As I mentioned at the beginning of the book, I primarily use the word "workshop" since I prefer a participatory style, allowing time for the participants to apply (or "workshop") the concepts to their own situation. Even if you plan to deliver a presentation that does not include a lot of participation from the audience, you still may need these skills anyway. In most cases, especially if you have a host, you may be asked to leave some time for questions at the end. This is a time to truly impress.

Having observed hundreds of trainers and facilitators over a couple of decades, I've realized that it's easy to impress or disappoint an audience with how you manage questions, discussions and group dynamics. It's not enough to just know your topic. To truly win over an audience, you will need to exercise social skills, along with facilitation and training skills.

The following pages offer some tips about facilitation and training skills including what to do and not do. They include how to prepare yourself mentally and emotionally beforehand, and how to be an excellent trainer and facilitator.

How to Prepare Yourself Mentally and Emotionally

You want to be able to comfortably describe your product or service (especially the results that your best clients achieve) with confidence and a natural feel. This may sound easy to you now, but so does riding a bike! It's not so easy until you know how and you've done it many times. If your product or service is still relatively new to you, then it's possible (and likely) you haven't yet had the chance to refine it and describe it many times. My suggestion is to get this practice before you deliver your workshop.

You also want to be able to comfortably describe your ideal clients with confidence and a natural feel. You can include what they most commonly wish for (in their own words), what they are good at, and what commonly gets in their way and impedes their success. Put yourself in their shoes and let them know you "get" them. The more you feel what that's like and can empathize with their situation, the easier it is for you to describe them. This is not easy to do until you are truly practiced at it. Again, my suggestion is to get this practice before you deliver your workshop.

How? It's best to practice this with others, rather than alone. You can get this type of practice at networking events or mastermind groups, and by meeting new people who ask about your work. Good networking groups for getting this type of practice are big enough, so not everyone knows each other already, and yet are small enough for everyone to make personal introductions. Conferences and other people's workshops are also good places to find that opportunity.

When you are comfortable and confident talking about your product or service, your ideal clients, your "Why," and showing your passion and personality, then it's time to practice your workshop with an audience. In the training world, it's called a pilot test.

Deliver pilot tests

Whenever possible, deliver your workshop as a pilot test (or a practice run) at least once and maybe twice, before any big, important opportunities to impress your most ideal clients and get your workshop just right! There is no shame in this. All good performers practice and rehearse – why wouldn't you?

Your goal for a pilot test is to be a learner of your own experiment. Although it is tempting to invite friends and family and willing supporters to your pilot test, I suggest, instead, that you fill your pilot test workshop with people who match your ideal clients as closely as possible. At a minimum, invite people who understand their problems or struggles, and who understand the intention and purpose of your workshop – to meet, impress and find new clients!

Here's an analogy: if you practice selling heaters to people in a place where it's never cold and they've never thought of buying one, they are not likely to truly understand the need for it or care much about spending money on one. They may tell you that they don't like the color or shape of the heaters you sell, but they may not ask questions about electric vs. gas powered, maintenance, efficiency, warranty, etc. If you are practicing selling heaters, you should do your pilot test for people who want and need heaters. Seems obvious, I know, but I've seen people fill up their pilot test with supportive, well-meaning friends, neighbors, and colleagues, who, unfortunately, despite good intentions, aren't very helpful.

For my pilot test, I personally invited five coaches, consultants and entrepreneurs (my ideal clients) to my home, and provided them lunch. Perhaps because I told them ahead of time that it was my pilot test, and I would ask them for their feedback, they were invested in my success. Not only did they provide great feedback, but a few of them attended my workshop again, once I had delivered it many times, recommended my workshop to others and became paying clients.

The more ideal prospects (or people who can easily relate to your ideal clients) that attend your pilot test, the better. That way, your pilot test is likely to be more effective at showing you what you couldn't see before. You may learn that the transitions from one phase of your workshop to another are clumsy. You may realize that when the participants make comments or ask you questions, fear shows up and derails you. A very common one is that you realize you've tried to pack too much into the time allotted and ran over schedule, or even had to skip the end – the all important end!

If the thought of practicing your workshop in front of your ideal clients makes you nervous, let them know this is just a practice run. Choose a few people from within the same eco-system as your ideal clients, and ask for their help. Explain the purpose of your workshop: to practice and receive their feedback. In my experience, most people are willing to help if and when they are asked. Plus, even though they're technically helping you, there's a high chance that they'll get value from it as well, so you're actually helping each other.

Invite and accept valuable feedback

When it comes time to receive feedback on the pilot test of your workshop, help people to help you. Ask for feedback that really counts – meaning it's substantial and valuable, rather than superficial. For example, feedback on the fonts or colors of your slides is fine, but ultimately not as impactful or valuable as feedback on the foundation and formula of your workshop.

If you choose to ask your pilot test audience for substantial feedback on your workshop, you can give them the following worksheet. This will help them help you. Before you give them this worksheet, however, and definitely before you receive their answers on the worksheet, check your own ability to accept valuable feedback.

I recommend that you pay attention to any defensiveness you may feel around the feedback. I can't emphasize this enough. Defensiveness inhibits your ability to learn, grow, and succeed. Be as open as possible to unlearn old, unneeded behaviors or beliefs, and to learn new, more productive ones.

When you are gracious about receiving candid feedback and truly interested in it, you will gain amazing insights about what your prospective clients value and want from you. In the process of receiving and accepting feedback, you are also building a relationship and trust with pilot workshop participants. Don't overlook the importance of that relationship, as these individuals could become advocates for you, they could feel more invested to help you promote your workshop or recommend it to their friends and colleagues.

Once you've offered your pilot test and received feedback, leave plenty of time for reflection and correction. Sometimes feedback from participants is not consistent with one another or they recommend something contrary to the advice in this book. It's understandable. They may not realize the differences that are required of a workshop that is meant to bring in clients rather than solely provide information.

Leave enough time to make the necessary changes, and even to offer a second pilot test to try out the changes – especially if they were substantial. Remember, a pilot test is very important. It's not just a practice round, it's meant for learning.

The following worksheet is actually for the participants of your pilot test, rather than you. You may want to give it to them prior to the workshop and explain why you are asking them these particular questions - to learn!

Worksheet:
Invite Valuable Feedback

Did the description at the beginning describe you, your struggles, challenges and desired future? If not, what was off base?

What did you learn that you didn't already know?

How could the workshop be even more valuable to you?

How would you describe what I'm selling and what the next steps are?

Do you see applications for my product or service that I didn't mention specifically?

How would you describe my training style?

Be as natural, self-confident and relaxed as possible.

Oooph! I'm humbled by how easy it is to write that last sentence, and yet how difficult it can be to achieve!

You may be asking yourself: *What is "natural" for me, anyway? What does "self-confident" or "relaxed" look like and feel like for me? When am I that way? How do I get there?*

It's worth the investment of time and self-reflection to know the answers to these questions. It's worth it for so many reasons. Possibly the most important reason is for you to be happy as a person, but also, specifically for the sake of delivering a workshop that brings in clients. If you're not sure how to answer them, it may be a good reason to work with a skilled life coach. Those are exactly the kinds of questions that a very good life coach could help you to explore.

As I learned from Fabienne Fredrickson, I truly believe that, as entrepreneurs, our number one job is to protect our confidence. While it's important to protect it every day, at all times, it's especially important to find your confidence and keep it during your workshop. An audience can "read" confidence, or lack of it! When you are not relaxed and self-confident, it doesn't matter what you say, people are more focused on your nervousness and your mistakes than on what you say. Besides, would you hire someone who doesn't seem confident at what they do?

One of the most obvious ways to become confident and relaxed, of course, is to be well prepared. All good performers rehearse. They don't all rehearse the same way though. Even though it may be tempting, please don't memorize a script or read from a script! I've seen both, and neither is very productive or effective.

One time, I helped one of my clients to practice her workshop, just before the first run of her new workshop. By the time we met, she had already spent a lot of time struggling to memorize her workshop script. She was working under the impression that she would be more polished and rehearsed if she had her script memorized. What happened, unfortunately, is that she didn't remember much, (she was too nervous to memorize) and instead, she felt unprepared, and scared for her first workshop.

Noticing that memorizing wasn't getting her the results she wanted, I advised her to change strategies and instead, write out index cards with only the main points and transitions of each section of her workshop. Yes, index cards may be an old-school way to do it (which doesn't mean it's any less effective), but let's not lose the lesson. The lesson here is to find the strategy that makes you most prepared, comfortable and effective.

Another time, I observed a client of mine practice his workshop before his big debut at a conference. He had the entire script of his workshop written out, word for word, and for 90-minutes, he read it directly from a three-ring binder. Fortunately, he had a theatre background and was incredibly entertaining and skilled at it. He read his script with very convincing intonation and inflection. His body language and hand gestures even fit what he was saying.

If I were hearing an audio file, or watching a theatre audition, it would have been perfectly entertaining and engaging. While it wasn't bad at all, he didn't seem natural to me. Unfortunately, the way he read his script from a binder makes a lot more sense at a theatre audition or for an audio book than it does for a live workshop. I wanted to see the natural him, not his theatre character or him playing the role of narrator.

As I said before, all good performers rehearse. They don't all rehearse the same way though. Since the pathway to confidence is different for everyone, it's more important that you learn what works for you. In a couple of pages, you'll find a worksheet that invites you to do this deep self-reflection.

Here a few ideas that have worked for me and some of my clients and may work for you, too. The objective of these ideas is to get us out of our overly active and usually self-critical mind (sometimes referred to as the "monkey brain") and, instead, to tap into the wisdom of our bodies. Our bodies naturally know more than many people give them credit for. The body gives off signals that we may not even hear or feel, if we don't pay attention. When we do pay attention, however, allowing the body to inform us, we can catch a momentary relief from our self-critical mind and feel more grounded and self-confident.

Breathe deeply and envision success

At a minimum, I recommend you do a deep breathing exercise each time you practice and especially right before you begin your workshop. It's as easy as lifting your arms up overhead, reaching up high, as you take the largest inhalation you can. Hold it for just a few seconds while you envision yourself confidently commanding the audience's attention and successfully expressing your genuine desire to help them. Then exhale slowly and deeply, paying attention to emptying your lungs as much as possible. If it helps, silently count to five as you exhale, slowing and pacing your breath with the counts. Repeat two more times.

You can always do this for yourself anytime and anywhere, or you can accept the help of a friend, close supporter, or life coach who knows how to calm you and leave you feeling grounded and confident.

Do physical activity and get fresh air

Take a walk, do some stretches, yoga or dancing. I recommend that you combine as much movement as you can, with as much fresh air as you can. Movement, fresh air and oxygen feed your whole body and your brain, allowing them to function at peak performance. I recommend that you set aside time in your day while you are preparing for your workshop and the day of your workshop for physical activity and fresh air. With this sacred time, do physical movement, preferably in silence or gently led, allowing yourself to envision your own success at your workshop. This may be the time to try a guided visioning exercise or meditation.

Again, you can always do this for yourself anytime and anywhere, or you can accept the help of a friend, close supporter, or life coach who knows how to calm you and leave you feeling grounded and confident. I also offer this service for my clients who are nervous before their workshop and they have said it's incredibly valuable.

Use the following worksheet to apply what you just read to your own situation. Since it will require clarity, I suggest you do some physical movement (a few stretches or maybe a short dance) and take in some fresh air before you begin. Your brain will appreciate the extra help!

Worksheet: Prepare for the Delivery of Your Workshop

What feels "natural" for you?

What does "self-confident" or "relaxed" look like and feel like for you?

When do you feel self-confident and relaxed?

How can you get yourself into a state of self-confidence and relaxation?

How do you maintain your composure in the midst of a challenging situation?

How to be an Excellent Presenter, Trainer, or Facilitator

To be effective as a trainer or facilitator of adults, you'll need to understand how adults learn. You'll also want to know how to facilitate experiential activities and discussions for adults. This all assumes, of course, that your ideal clients are adults.

Training Adults

Adults prefer a learning environment where they **feel valued** and respected for their experiences. As a trainer you should ask participants to share their stories. Be sure to give positive reinforcement when they contribute.

Adults prefer **learning to be active** rather than passively sitting and listening to you. It is important that you give your participants opportunities to participate in a variety of activities such as discussions, problem-solving case studies, or brainstorming.

Adults will be **actively engaged in learning** if they can see how the training will meet their needs. As a trainer it is important to identify your participants' learning needs, and to explain how the training content will be of benefit to them.

Adults want to **direct their own learning**. Provide opportunities for participants to make choices so that they can decide which skills they want and need to learn.

Adults have **varied learning styles**. Some adults learn best visually, others learn best by listening and still others by doing. Use a variety of training methods in order to accommodate all learning styles.

Adults learn new content when it relates to something they already know. **Link new content to existing content** by analogies or stories.

Adults appreciate having an opportunity to **apply what they have learned** as soon as possible. Make sure to give all participants a chance to practice new skills.

Adults will learn and remember content when it is **reinforced with repetition**. Try to repeat key concepts, but vary the context if possible, to show different applications.

Adults are motivated by **positive encouragement**. Be sure to reward your participants with positive feedback and express appreciation when they participate.

The **adult attention span is between 8 and 12 minutes**. Change the pace of the activity every 8 minutes. Change the activity every 20 minutes. Take a "bio-needs" or movement break every 60-90 minutes.

Facilitating experiential activities and discussion among adults

Once you understand how adults learn, you're more likely to include experiential activities and discussion in your workshop.

Experiential activities really help to make training active. It is often far better and more effective for participants to experience something rather than to hear it talked about. I recommend activities that give the participants the chance to try what you are suggesting, first, so that they will learn more, and second, so that questions will emerge and discussion will follow.

The following steps will help to make your experiential activities a success.

1. Explain your objectives. Participants like to know what is going to happen and why.

2. Sell the benefits. Explain why you are doing the activity and how the activity connects with any preceding activities.

3. Speak slowly when giving directions and provide visual backup. Make sure the instructions are understood before you ask people to begin.

4. Demonstrate the activity if the directions are complicated. Let the participants see the activity in action before they do it.

5. If using small groups, divide participants into subgroups before giving further directions. If you do not, participants may forget the instructions while the sub-groups are being formed.

6. Inform participants how much time they have. State the time you have allotted for the entire activity and then periodically announce how much time remains.

7. Keep the activity moving. Don't slow things down by endlessly recording participant contributions on flip charts or blackboards and don't let a discussion drag on for too long.

8. Challenge the participants. More energy is created when activities generate a moderate level of tension. If tasks are a snap, participants will get lethargic.

9. Always discuss the activity. When an activity has concluded, invite participants to process their feelings or reactions, and share their insights and learnings.

Your role during a group discussion is to facilitate the flow of questions and comments from participants. You can also use the opportunity to help participants advance their learning by getting them to think more deeply about their comments and questions. You can also tie their comments back to the content of your workshop, demonstrating your expertise and gaining credibility.

If, at any point, you are asked a question that you're not sure how to answer, you can ask the group if they have encountered this situation before and invite them to respond. This invites group discussion, enables others to share their expertise, and also (if you need it) buys you some time to think of an answer. In some cases, it's building on the answer(s) that other participants provide.

Some of my clients have shown a resistance to facilitating open discussions. It's true, with group discussions, come some risks. If you're not careful or not skilled at facilitating discussions, it's possible that the discussion can get out of control. If this happens, you may lose a valuable opportunity to follow your own plans for the workshop, and you may also lose credibility.

Here are some tips for maintaining control and facilitating discussions among adults:

- Paraphrase what a participant has said so that he or she feels understood and so that the other participants can hear a concise summary of what has been said.

- Check your understanding of a participant's statement or ask the participant to clarify what he or she is saying.

- Compliment an interesting or insightful comment.

- Elaborate on a participant's contribution to the discussion with examples, or suggest a new way to view the problem.

- Energize a discussion by quickening the pace, using humor, or, if necessary, prodding the group for more contributions.

- Disagree (gently) with a participant's comments to stimulate further discussion.

- Mediate differences of opinion between participants and relieve any tensions that may be brewing.

- Pull together ideas, showing their relationship to each other.

- Change the group process by altering the method for obtaining participation or by having the group evaluate ideas that have been presented.

- Summarize (and record, if desired) the major views of the group.

Now that you've learned how to deliver a workshop that addresses the immediate needs of your clients, the next step is to stay in touch with interested participants beyond the workshop so that they transition from thinking about buying your product or service to actually doing so.

PART 5:
THE CONVERSION

After one of my workshops, a woman introduced herself and said, "I'd like to work with you. I already have a workshop that I know is great. I get a good crowd every time, and people are really engaged and thankful for it. The problem is that nobody converts into a client afterwards."

One month later, we had our first coaching session together and we reviewed her workshop materials and how she delivers it. The reason she wasn't getting clients from her workshop became immediately clear to me. She wasn't doing anything to move the participants down her sales funnel.

She didn't provide the participants her business card, since she said her contact information was on her handout and so she didn't see a need. She didn't use a sign-in sheet, so she didn't know anyone's names, have any contact information or any demographic information about them either. She didn't provide them any guidance or "call to action" about what to do next. She had no way to stay in touch with them. Doh!

You must be proactive!

In my experience, the workshop and "Follow-Up Free Opt-In," are extremely important, but not always sufficient. They are often enough, when there is beautiful alignment between you and a participant of your workshop. Some people, however, are not ready at that very moment to make a decision to work with you. They may need more experience of you and the value you can provide before they are ready to commit and spend any money with you.

To capitalize on those who want to work with you, but aren't quite ready, you must follow up with them after the workshop. Not just once, and not just by email. If you want them to grow, you must provide water and sunshine to the seeds you planted.

To get the participants' contact information and their permission to use it, is already a win in and of itself. In this age of email overload, most people don't easily give out their contact information. If you get their email address (or even better), all their contact information, including a phone number and address, you are in a much stronger position to follow up with them and convert them into paying clients.

How to Follow Up with Your Prospects After the Workshop

If you've prepared the end of your workshop, following the suggestions covered in Part 2: The Formula, then you already have the reason (and permission) to be in touch with the participants of your workshop at least once, and preferably over time. This reason is to provide them something of enormous value that they need and want in that moment: the "Follow-Up Free Opt-In".

At the end of your workshop, describe the value and the benefits that people will get from your "Follow-Up Free Opt-In." Those who are ready to work with you right away may not necessarily need it to make their decision. Others have reasons why they aren't ready right away. Maybe it's financial or logistical, or it could be for an infinite variety of other reasons. Regardless of the reason, you need a proactive strategy for keeping in touch in both the short and long-term.

Follow-up in the short-term

First, let's look at how to be in touch with your participants in the short-term. Here's a method that has worked nicely for me, and my clients who have tried it. While still at the workshop, you ask people to indicate their interest in having a conversation with you about how you could help them. You could do this a variety of ways. Here's the way I do it. It's a little bit old school, but it works. That's what you want – an easy process that works.

When I ask for participants' business cards in exchange for the "Follow-Up Free Opt-In," I also ask them to put a star on the card if they would like me to call them to talk about their situation or answer any questions. That's a quick and easy way for them to indicate that they are curious and interested enough in the topic to make more time for me. Those who do it have made yet another move down the sales funnel.

This conversation could be by phone or in person, but it's critical that it happen very quickly - meaning within

2-3 days of your workshop, while the topic (and you) are still very fresh in their minds.

Whenever I suggest this, my clients respond with some version of "What will we talk about?" Relax. Let them tell you what they need. Your first job is to be genuinely interested in them and to stay curious about their situation. Your second job is to be prepared for the many possible paths that the conversation could take. We'll look at a couple of paths the conversation could take, but first let's get clear on what it means to be genuinely interested and curious.

When you are genuinely interested in your prospects, then you don't push yourself on them and feel "salesy". Instead, you aim to understand what they are going through by inviting them to share their situation. The questions you might ask them could include:

- I'm curious, please tell me about your situation.
- What's working and not working for you?
- What's that like? or What's the impact of that?
- What would you like to be different six months from now?

When you are genuinely interested in your prospects, you naturally use your active listening skills and show more empathy for their situation. You relinquish expectations and avoid jumping to conclusions. You show patience and understanding of the difficulties they are experiencing. <u>You ask about them, and do not dominate by talking about yourself. This is important.</u> This conversation is not necessarily a time to talk about yourself or your products or services, or prices, or anything related to sales. And, at the same time, it could be. It depends on the path that the conversation takes.

As I said, your second job is to be prepared for the many possible paths the conversation could take. When you hear the answers to these questions, it will be much easier to tell if this person shares the characteristics (positive attributes or struggles) of your ideal clients - the ones you described in Part 1: The Foundation.

If this person does not seem to fit the profile of your ideal clients, then I recommended you get curious about why they have asked you to call. The questions you might ask them could include:

- What did you get from the workshop?
- What was helpful about the workshop for you?
- How can I be helpful to you now?

On the other hand, if this person does seem to fit the profile of your ideal clients, then I recommend you have a plan for inviting him or her to work with you, or buy your product or service. This could be your opportunity to close the sale. Be prepared for it. On the following pages, you will find suggestions for how to close the sale.

Now, let's look at how to be in touch with your participants in the long-term.

Follow-up in the long-term

While it would be fantastic for business if the participants of our workshops converted into clients right away, they are not always ready in that very moment. Instead, we face some common challenges such as these:

- prospects want to buy our product or service, but can't afford them now;

- prospects want to buy our product or service, but need to get other things finished or prepared first;

- prospects make it very difficult to stay in touch because they don't respond to e-mails or voice mails.

Because of these challenges, some very valid questions come up, like:

- How do you stay in touch without coming across as trying to make a sale, especially when the prospects have indicated that they are not ready to buy?

- How frequently should you be in touch and about what?

- How do you know when to continue to pursue a prospect when they are not being responsive and when to cut your losses and move on?

The answers to these questions help provide you with a strategy for following-up in the long term. They are the basis for your marketing strategy. You'll likely need a marketing strategy, if you don't have one already. And, you'll likely need to implement it, consistently and as often as possible.

If you are looking for extra help in this area, I recommend hiring a marketing coach, and reading the many great marketing strategy books out there. For coaches, consultants and entrepreneurs like us, who look for our own clients, having a great understanding of practical marketing tools, combined with a well-thought out marketing strategy is essential.

Use the following worksheet to apply what you just read to your own situation. Since it will require clarity, I suggest you do some physical movement (a few stretches or maybe a short dance) and take in some fresh air before you begin. your brain will appreciate the extra help.Your brain will appreciate the extra help!

Worksheet:
Your Strategy for Staying in Touch and Relevant

What is your method for keeping in touch with people in the short-term?

When you have a phone conversation with your prospects, what questions will you ask them?

What is your strategy for keeping people engaged with you in the long-term?

What systems do you need to set up for yourself to ensure that you stay in touch with your prospects and stay relevant to them over time?

How to Close the Sale

At the beginning of any conversation with your prospects, I recommend you seek to understand their current situation -including what's working and not working. This way you will have a much better sense if that person (or people, or organization) matches the characteristics of your ideal clients. If and when this is the case, then you want to show him or her that you understand the struggles or obstacles he or she is experiencing, and that you care. It's important that you actually do care! That makes you a much better listener.

Demonstrate you were listening carefully by paraphrasing back to the person what you heard. Be careful not to insert any of your own judgment, attachment or interpretation, but rather check for understanding. If the person that you're speaking to is, in fact, someone that you can help, and you genuinely believe that they could get great results from your product or service, then you could reassure them of that (which they likely already suspect) by saying something like "I can absolutely help you with that!" then pause.

To pause is advice that I got when I first learned to close the sale. When you create a pause in the conversation, you allow some space for the person to ask for more information about how you can help them. When they ask that, then your job is to explain your product or service. As I mentioned above, you want to describe the results that people get with your product or service first. Once they have indicated that they do want those results, then you can describe the process for how you'll get them there.

This is your chance to confidently describe the details they may not have heard yet (with enough, but not too much detail). You also want to include the price. Then pause again and take a deep breath. This moment is very hard for many people in the early days of their business. Just breathe! When you are truly confident that you can help this person to get great results, then this part of the conversation is easier.

Research shows us that many people rely heavily on their thinking, judging, ego-laden mind to make decisions. Yet, our bodies have so much wisdom. It's best to get people out of their (sometimes overly) analytical and critical, self-sabotaging minds and encourage them to check in with the wisdom of their body for making this decision. At this point, you could ask the person what their gut feeling is. Listen carefully, as their gut is likely right. At least, their gut reaction is an interesting observation point. Then get curious again and continue to show you care. It's important that you actually do care!

If and when this person sounds like a match and you are still confident that you can help this person get great results, then invite them to work with you. If and when this person agrees, then congratulate him or her and show that you genuinely believe he or she made a smart decision – even if it was a gut decision. Explain your start-up process, including a contract or agreement, any welcome materials, invoices, and if possible, take their deposit or full payment in that moment.

Although I don't specifically address it in this book, you will need to lay the groundwork for actually converting your prospects into clients. You will likely need a contract or agreement, an invoicing system, a bookkeeping system, a place to work with them, a follow-up system, and any other system that may be required by your specific product or service.

Similar to creating your workshop, the actual process of converting clients will show you what systems you need in place to make your business function efficiently and effectively. Don't let a simple logistical element (like not having a way to receive their payments) catch you off guard and potentially communicate to your new clients that you aren't fully prepared or ready to receive them. Be ready to receive your clients once you've converted them.

Here's an example of how this "closing the sale" conversion happens for me sometimes. Not all the time, but sometimes, it happens this easily.

On the morning of what I'll call day one, I delivered a free, 90-minute, face-to-face workshop, at a co-working space in my neighborhood. There were eight people there – a few business coaches, a couple of technology consultants, a couple of writers / editors and a health coach.

Near the very end of the workshop, I used the technique that I described in Part 2: The Formula, of offering to send the participants my "Follow-Up Free Opt-In" called "The Foundation and The Formula to Deliver Workshops that Bring in Clients". To receive this free resource, I asked for their business card in exchange. I showed them a hard copy of the free resource and described the benefits of it. I also said that I would add them to my subscriber list, which means that they receive free video blogs from me. I described the value of my video blogs, being full of tips, tricks and resources specifically about how to deliver a workshop that brings in clients. Finally, I also offered the quick and easy option to put a star on their business card if they would like me to call them in the next two days to talk about their workshop.

That afternoon, I entered all of the new email addresses that I had earned that day into my subscriber list and sent them an email. In this email, I thanked them for coming to the workshop and provided the link to download the "Follow-Up Free Opt-In" from my website. I scheduled time in my calendar in the next two days to call the people who had put stars on their business cards (which were six out of the eight people there).

The next day, day two, I called one of the women who had put a star on her business card. After a few minutes to get to know each other, our conversation went like this:

Me: "Tell me about your business."

Her: She explained that her business is going well already. She has given multiple presentations and workshops at conferences already and loves to teach and train people. At the same time, she has noticed herself gaining enthusiasm and energy for something other than how she's earning most of her income. She'd like to help people who are interested in pursuing the same kind of career that she has, but don't know how to get started. She is not trying to grow her business to be larger, but rather she wants to shift it slightly, allowing her to pursue more of what has already grabbed her attention – helping "newbies".

We continued to talk about that and how she could use a workshop to find prospects that fit her new interest and bring in a new, different kind of client that way. After about fifteen minutes, our conversation went like this:

Me: "So, as I understand it, you.... (and I described back to her what I had heard) and then said "Did I get that right?"

Her: "You did!"

Me: "Well, that's absolutely do-able!" (I paused and waited).

Her: "Will you tell me more about what it's like to work with you?"

Me: I started by describing the results that she could get from working with me. Then I described my three workshop coaching programs, including the price of each. Then I said "Hypothetically, if you knew that you wanted to work together, which program would be the best fit for you?"

Her: She said that the middle package sounded right for her needs and schedule.

Me: "Fantastic! Would you like to work together?"

Her: "Sure! Let's do it."

Me: "Congratulations! You just made a great choice."

Then I said I'd send her the written agreement for us both to sign and an invoice to get started. She quickly agreed to both and so we set a date to get started with our first session in two weeks.

We hung up the phone after about 45 minutes and I sent her the agreement and the invoice. She sent them both back to me right away and I thanked her. By day seven, we were officially working together.

Meanwhile, on day three and eight, I sent more reminders to the other participants of that workshop about the "Follow-Up Free Opt-In" I had sent them. Included in these email reminders were videos of me describing the value of the offer and how they can get the most out of it. The data from my subscriber list provider shows that six of the eight people opened the email, clicked through to the video and downloaded the "Follow Up Free Opt-In".

This is how it can happen. Again, it doesn't always happen that easily, but it when it does, it feels great! By following the methods in this book, you'll be working towards conversations like this one becoming a regular part of your business.

A Note From the Author

Thank you for taking time to read this book. I hope you have found a lot of value in it.

By reading this book, and filling in the worksheets, you may have noticed that you lack some clarity about your decisions and so designing your own workshop has proven difficult. Please do not feel bad about this! It's normal. And, I can help you.

I've created workshop coaching programs uniquely designed just for you, no matter where you live. You may find a course on presentation skills, facilitation skills or instructional design, but not this. Working either in-person or virtually, I help you design the right signature workshop (of any topic and length) that brings in clients to your business.

If you're considering getting more help on your workshop, here's an exercise to help.

1. Count out six months from now. What month and year is that? Write that down here:

   _____

2. How much money would you like to be making in your business by that date? Write that down here: _____

3. Estimate how much you would (realistically) make from working with one client. Write that down here: _____

4. Calculate how many new clients it would take to reach your six-month financial goal? Write that down here: _____

5. Consider this number of clients. Have you been able to find (and enroll) that many clients without the right signature workshop in the last six months? Write your response here:

_____

If you realize that getting professional and expert help on your signature workshop is crucial to the success of your business, please visit my website at www.lesliezucker.com for more information about my workshop coaching programs.

With the right signature workshop, plenty of preparation, and a lot of justified confidence, your workshop can be a very rewarding way to grow your business. That's what I want for you!

In this dance of life together,

Leslie Zucker

References

Broad, Mary, Newstrom J. W. Transfer of Training. (Reading, MA: Addison Wesley, 1992)

Fredrickson, Fabienne. The Client Attraction System. (Client Attraction, LLC, 2012)

Glasser, William. Choice Theory Psychology. (1965)

K. Patricia Cross Adults as Learners: Increasing Participation and Facilitating Learning (San Francisco: Jossey-Bass, 1982)

Knowles, Malcolm S. The Adult Learner an Adult Species. (Houston: Gulf Publishing Company: Jossey-Bass, 1990)

Knox, Alan B. Helping Adults Learn: A Guide to Planning, Implementing, and Conducting Programs. (San Francisco: Jossey-Bass, 1986)

Kolb, D. A. Experiential Learning. (Englewood Cliffs, NJ: Prentice Hall, 1984)

Miller, Lori E. The WOW Factor – 7 Secrets to Great Presentations (Lulu Press, 2015)

Perl Berman, Beth. 7 Win-Wins For Your Business When You Know Your WHY. (BPB Solutions, LLC, 2015)

Pike, Bob. Creative Training Techniques Handbook (Amherst, MA: HRD press, 2003)

Silberman, Mel. ASTD Team & Organization Development Sourcebook (ASTD Press, 2005)

About the Author

Leslie Zucker teaches self-employed coaches, consultants and entrepreneurs around the world how to consistently deliver workshops that bring in clients, so they save time and effort, make a HUGE positive impact in the world, all while making more money in their business.

Leslie created the system "How to Deliver Workshops that Bring in Clients™", the proven step-by-step process that shows self-employed coaches, consultants and entrepreneurs exactly how to convert audiences and participants into clients with authenticity and confidence. Through her workshops, presentations and coaching programs, Leslie shows her clients how to create a rewarding business and love being their own boss!

As a sought-after public speaker for The Power Conference, The Maryland Women's Business Center, The Chesapeake Bay Organizational Development Network, The Association of Talent Development, We Work, Impact Hub, General Assembly, and Creative Colony, Leslie has grown her own business using the same, no nonsense, step-by-step methodology that she teaches.

Leslie has a confident, fun, fast-paced and informal presence that engages audiences from 3 to 300 – in both English and Spanish. She is quick to involve people, and provide opportunities for people to apply what they've learned to their own situation. Her style mixes the practical how-to, delivered with a dose of inspiration and motivation. As a result, she provides real value, and facilitates "aha!" moments for both beginners and established business owners.

Through her video blogs, free gifts, online presence, and coaching, Leslie reaches and inspires hundreds of people. She currently lives in Washington, DC, loves to take long walks in Rock Creek Park with her dog, grow vegetables in her backyard, cook healthy food, travel internationally and spend as much time as possible dancing and talking about life and awareness with her partner.

Connect With the Author

If you've enjoyed this book, wouldn't you like to see the author deliver her own signature workshop? It's called "Deliver Workshops That Bring in Clients.™."

You can book Leslie Zucker to speak at conferences, retreats, professional development groups, networking events, coaching courses, consulting firms, co-working spaces, anywhere full of people who are responsible for marketing themselves and finding their own clients.

www.lesliezucker.com

www.deliverworkshopsthatbringinclients.com

info@lesliezucker.com

@DCWorkshopWoman

facebook.com/lesliezuckertrainingandcoaching

linkedin.com/in/lesliezucker

More Resources from the Author

On www.lesliezucker.com, sign up to receive even more worksheets, examples, tips and tricks about delivering workshops that bring in clients.

Notes and Questions for the Author

Notes and Questions for the Author

34905428R00068

Made in the USA
Middletown, DE
09 September 2016